THE ALPHABETICAL ZOO

THE

ALPHABETICAL

ZOO

BY GEORGE BARKER

ILLUSTRATED BY KRYSTYNA ROLAND

FABER AND FABER
3 QUEEN SQUARE
LONDON

874817

First published in 1972
by Faber and Faber Limited
3 Queen Square, London WC1
Printed in Great Britain by
Clarke, Doble & Brendon Ltd, Plymouth
ISBN 0 571 09892 4   All rights reserved

CONTENTS

Runes and Rhymes and Tunes and Chimes
To Aylsham Fair

for Raffaella-Flora

When upon the Human Face
the Goblin turns his grinning gaze
he thinks: "O what a parody!
There, but for the Grace of God, goes me!"

APE

I am the Ape and I can climb
   straight up the tallest wall,
up flagpoles, maypoles and North Poles,
   yes, anything at all
that's vertical, horizontal or
   even diagonal.
I never hesitate because
   if I did I would fall.
I swing from branch to branch of trees
   so sickeningly tall
that I could look down far upon
   St Paul's Cathedral
and spit a little bit of spittle
   upon the Dome of Paul.
Yes, far below me I survey
   a world so very small
that I could take it in my hand
   like a little rubber ball —
O I must be the Principal
   and Primate of it all.
I am the Ape, the highest and
   the cleverest animal.

BEE

I buzz, I buzz, I buzz
because I am a Bee.
I never rest
in my own nest
except when I've
filled up a hive
with *excelicious* Honey.
From West Ealing
to Darjeeling
no other creature can
produce one jot
or tiny spot
of my divine confection:
no, not for love
or health or wealth
no, sir, not even for money
can any factory
make satisfactory
natural Norfolk honey.

From this you see
that I, the Bee,
by natural selection
am cleverer than
machines or man
and very near perfection.

COW

I am the Cow
of pastures green
crowned with flowers
to show I am Queen.
I am so placid
and so serene
I rule the entire
pastoral scene.
My eyes are like
lustrous carbuncles
(my nose is like roses
set in between)
and more elegant ankles
you have never seen
and the curl at my forehead
like the pearl of a Queen.

My horns are like ivory,
my tail is like silk—
O Silly Bee, Silly Bee,
so silly, so funny,
what on earth is your honey
without my milk?

DOG

Dog I am dog;
at dawn and at dark
I rule with my masterly
bite and bark.
Who's there? Who?
Come out. Speak
if you're a man.
If mouse, squeak.
I stand fourfooted,
foursquare. Mark,
Stranger, my ferocious bark,
and my red eye in
the dangerous dark.
I am the housedog,
I am the hound
on hearth and hill,
I rule all around
and the rat and the mouse
and the cat in the dark
cower and tremble
at my bark.
I am the King
of the – Catalogue?
No. I am the King
of the Dogalogue.
I am the Big Chief
Running Dog.

ELEPHANT

Elephants are elephants
the way mountains are mountains
the way palaces are palaces
and railway trains railway trains.
There is absolutely
no point whatever
in denying that Elephants
are extremely clever.
When an Elephant retreats
he places his foot
backwards where it
was formerly put
because a retreating
Elephant knows
he was safe when he came
so he's safe when he goes.

The Elephant dances
more lightly than
any other mastodon
can can-can.
Indeed the tremendous
Elephant
does everything
other animals can't
such as turn his nose
into a hose
or—(no magician's
a cleverer fellah!)—
his ear into
an umbrella.

He's a house on the ground
that can stroll about,
he's an island in water
when his back sticks out,
he's stronger than towers
built of bricks and mortar,
he can carry a trunk
like a railway porter,
he's the Lord of Peace
and the Lord of Slaughter,
and he's gentle as
a Ranee's daughter
and if you don't love him,
well, you oughta.

FOX

Foxes frolic over fences
when the Hunt is up,
selling Masters of Foxhounds what we
technically call a pup.
I too have seen the view halloo
following in full cry
straight to the East as, to the West,
the lazy fox trots by.
I have even heard of foxes that
would sit with their legs crossed
looking like red-haired farmhands whose
faces were sharp with frost,
advising packs of hounds how to
pick up the scent they'd lost.
The Fox enjoys the knowledge that
he can outwit the Hunt.
He does this simply: he just turns
everything back to front
and when they go to Huntingdon
he goes to Ding Dong Hunt.

GOOSE

Golden Goose, Golden Goose,
    shed me a feather
and I will keep it in
a money box of tin
    or purse of leather.

O if all geese were gold
    we would want many:
but when a beggar begs
better to give him eggs
    than a gold penny.

I have a silly goose
    not made of gold.
She is so fat and fine
this silly wife of mine
    she'll never be sold.

HORSE

Heigh Ho the Hobby Horse
   Piebald or Grey
(I did not know that Grey is White
   but so the horsemen say,)
Strawberry Roan or Black
   or a Dirty Dun —
Every horse has invisible wings,
   yes, every one.

There's the Flat Racer,
the Steeplechaser
and the Great Grey Cavalry Charger;
and there is, of course,
the Rodeo Horse
like a jumping flea, only larger.

There's the handy Pony
from Tony Pandy
and the Milkman's Horse with the hat on;
and the Hunter who
bruised me so blue
I wondered what I had sat on.

There's that Rapscallion
the Wild White Stallion,
and no one, no one, can tame him.
At the sight of a rein
he's off like a train
to the green hills and who can blame him?

O for the furious
perhaps injurious
racing over the mountains and heather!
with the bridle loose
and stirrups no use
and everything hell for leather!

I have a Rocking Horse, and his
     name is Dapple Grey
and he and I will jump a ditch
and win the Race Cesarewitch
     one memorable day.

IBIS

The Ibis is a sacred Bird
   and lives beside the Nile.
She looks just like the letter S
and eats the eggs – with watercress –
   of the great Crocodile.

The Ibis is a sacred Bird:
   her neck is long and black.
If taken from the River Nile
she dies in a little while
   of pining to go back.

JAY

Jays are birds
just of words.
They chatter
and natter
about any old matter
or about nothing at all.
I cannot dissemble
that in this they resemble
almost everybody I know:
like so many people
who are mentally feeble
they loudly say nothing at all.

KANGAROO

Who are you
Kangaroo?
Are you
an Emu   *clothes*
clad in the habit
of a vertical
Australian Rabbit?
When hunters pursue   *chase*
You, Kangaroo,
Why do you do
What you do?
Do you
know what you do?
Why, Kangaroo,
this is what you do
when the hunters
pursue you: *chase*
You stand up
from your slouch
and remove
from your pouch
your Baby
so small
(one inch
over all)

yes, at a pinch
without flicker
or flinch
your Kangaroo Babe
you cast away
into Woomerong Waste
or Botany Bay
and with a bound
you springboard up

and leapfrog away,
and your Kangaroo Babe
is later found
like a little finger
on the ground.
O Kangaroo
what a thing to do!
No wonder there are
so few of you!

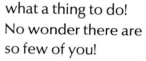

LAMB

I am the Lamb that whickers
  out of a cloud of dreams
I am the changeling of spring places
  and fields and freshet streams
I am as white as Winter was
  and as Love seems.

I jump up into the bright air
  of the April day
so that to me the world will seem
  one moment far away
and then I can leap back on it
  as it goes on its way.

I am the Lamb, the Lamb of Love,
  as holy as the child.
I am the lost black lamb on whom
  the Morning Shepherd smiled.
I lie down with the Lion and
  we slumber in the wild.

MARMOSET

The Marmoset cannot forget
    the jungles whence it came.
The Marmoset, when locked in cages
foams at the mouth and rants and rages,
    unteachably untame.

All Zoos should let the Marmoset
    return to jungles. Then
in every Marmosetless Zoo
a Marmosetful hullaballoo
    would never be heard again.

When in a pet the Marmoset
    erects its bushy tail
and in a Marmosetic fit
will beat itself to death with it
    if other methods fail.

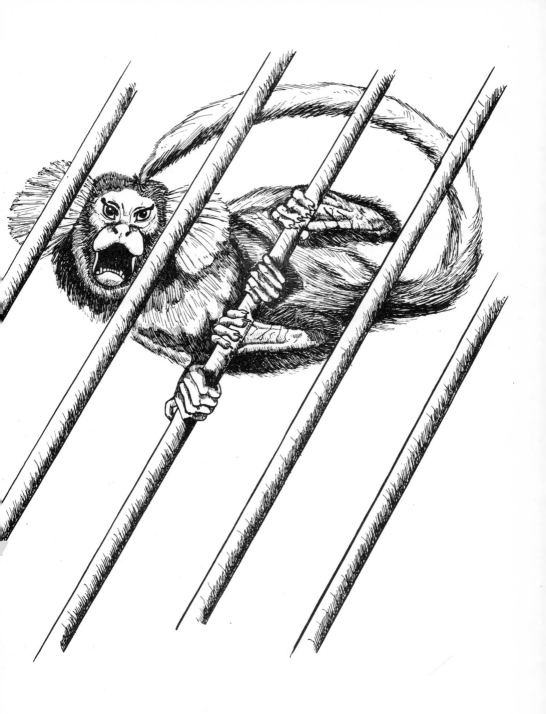

NIGHTINGALE

Nightingale, Nightingale,
    O tell me, why is it
you pay to my wood such
    a flying, a vanishing,
    a fleeting visit,
for, Nightingale, Nightingale,
    it seems as though
you no sooner come to me
    than you go.
I hear you whispering
    and whistling on
and on through the night
    and then you are gone.
Where can you fly to
    that loves you more than
my wood and my garden and
    my Maytime can?
Ah, Nightingale, Nightingale,
    too briefly bereft
is the Valley of Thessaly
    that you have left!

Recalling the cascades
    and waterfalls and
shepherds and sheepdogs of
    your native land,
O Nightingale, little brown
    Syrinx of sorrow,
take Sussex to Thessaly
    with you tomorrow!

OX

The Ox is an honest beast
   who once pulled the plough.
Today the engine reaps and sows.
   What does the Ox do now?

The Ox stands silently beside
   fields that the tractor turns
and for the ploughman's hand and voice
   fiercely the dumb Ox yearns.

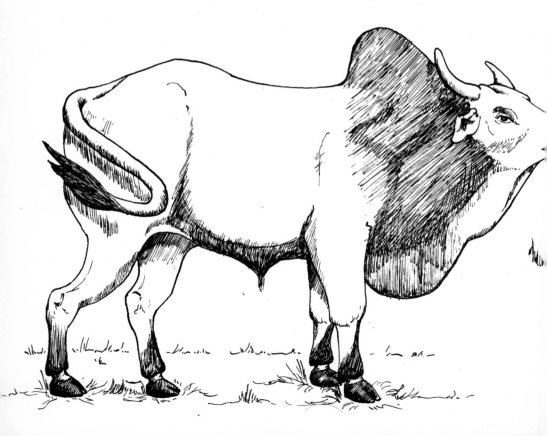

PUMA

Within the Puma's golden head
    burn Jungle, flames and paradises.
And all who look into his red
and fiery eye by fury fed
    the Puma paralyses.

The Sun, the Orchid and the Snake
    like demons of the Bible
rage in his brow. The earthquake
and the volcanic mountain shake
    and tremble in his eyeball.

QUAIL

The Quail and the Partridge
went out to shoot one day.
Said the Partridge to the Quail:
"Observe my short and silly tale.
Within your Castle's cosy kitchen
I have left all my ammunition
I am ashamed to say."
The Quail replied: "Dear Mr Partridge,
within my pocket lies one cartridge.
Will you accept it, pray?"

Anticipating, then, the thrill
of one single little kill
the Partridge, with a smile,
answered: "Why, of course I will."
The Quail loaded that one cartridge
and in the neatest style
shot his bosom friend the Partridge
before they'd gone a mile.

The aristocratic Partridge
said: "I accept that cartridge.
I thank you for your kindness
And go to meet my God."
The Quail said: "My dear Partridge
to perish for one cartridge
is surely rather odd?"

"I know of nothing better,"
said the Partridge. "Go and get a
marble slab and write upon it
my commemoratory Sonnet."
The Quail was not a Sonneteer
and so I write this Ballad here.
Yes, it was I, with my last cartridge
shot my dear friend Mr Partridge
who did not die of roundshot. He
died for this bit of Poetry.

RHINOCEROS

Rhinoceroses do not sing
   Beside the River Rhine.
Rhinemaidens do. They break the heart.
   But — I regret — not mine.

Rhinemaidens happen to believe
   that all who hear them sing
will with them in Eternal Love
   be bound in a Wagoner's ring.

Myself I doubt if this is true.
   The Rhinemaidens I have seen
were simply rather healthy girls
   wet, fat, and very clean.

But – this the wise Chinee well knows –
   Rhinoceroses' horns
reduced to powder and mixed with wine
   not only cure your corns

But of all potions of True Love
   the powdered horn of the Rhino
is without exception the very perfection
   if mixed with a little wine-o.

I think that all who fall in love
   with Rhinemaidens at dawn
must have sat down to a breakfast of
   powdered Rhinoceros horn.

SNAKE

I, the reptilian,
serpentine, jewel-eyed,
golden-scaled, spiralling
splendour of Snake,
I in the shallows of
Nigers and Amazons
I dream of Death
when I sleep, when I wake.
I bind the Bird and
the Beast and
all creatures in
my coiled fascination
no Lion could break.

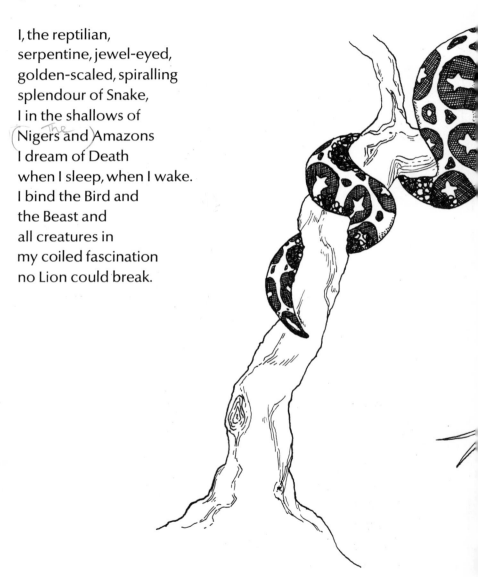

I am the Python,
the Great Anaconda,
I am the Cobra the
King of Golconda,
I am the Winged, the
Plumed Aztec Serpent,

I am the Rainbow
that climbs in the tree,
I am the Kiss of Death,
the hiss of Darkness.
I and I only
do not fear me.

TURTLE DOVE

The Turtle and the Turtle Dove
  once upon a time
sat down together on a rock
   making up a rhyme.

"The Turtle," said the Turtle Dove,
  "delights to eat the Myrtle
in which I live. Shall I, a Dove,
  be eaten by a Turtle?"

"The Turtle Dove," replied the Turtle,
  "is an untruthful bird.
It is neither a Turtle nor Dove.
  Each is the wrong word."

"Well, come to that," said the Turtle Dove,
  "look where the truth has brought us.
If I am not a Turtle Dove,
  Well, Turtle, you're a Tortoise."

UNICORN

When the Unicorn descends from the Hartz Mountains
    it is always the time of full Moon.
Down, then, through dappled shadows and woods like curtains
down through the spangling moonlight and falling silver triangles,
    it picks its way over the snow
    it pricks its way through the gloom
Of those murmuring conifers the glimmering firs
    lifting its ivory horn
As it steps twisting down the moon-littered stairs
    of stones and crystal leaves
    following its star-anointed
    and dawn-pointed horn,
and the white moonlight shakes and shivers on its sides
    as it leaps and turns and slides
down through dark glades and by fountaining cascades
down between the mountain walls and by bright waterfalls
    flickering like an antlered prince
    in the Austrian moonlight.

When the Unicorn descends from the Hartz Mountains
  through woods and snow
  in the light of the Moon
  and winter stars, does it go
  following its star-pointing horn
  in search of its first dawn?
  Is it seeking the bright morn
  of the day it will be born?
O where does the descending Unicorn go?

VULTURE

Veering and wheeling
high in the ceiling
of the Sahara sky
I can tell a bone
from a whitewashed stone
with my telescopic eye.

I look like a witch
flown up out of a ditch
dishevelled and dirty but never-
the-less horrifying,
for I eat the dying
and dead who are with me for ever.

My hooked beak is like
a scythe or a spike
for tearing the flesh from the skeleton.
My skin is as hoary
as the Old Hermit's story
or the filthy old paper they tell it on.

I love offal and scrag
or a bit of old rag
and for sweets I eat eyeballs of camels;
the most delicious
of edible dishes
for me is the dead flesh of mammals.

Vulture on high
I watch heroes die
as they fail to traverse the Sahara;
I drop like a wreath
on their bones underneath,
then I place their false teeth
on my bald head like a tiara.

WARBLERS

Blackcap, whitethroat, chiff-chaff, small
    insectivorous songbirds, my dear,
warblers of willow, sedge, reed, wood – all
    return in the Spring to sing here.

Then in due season but for no apparent reason
    they fly back to the shores of Africa.
O why do whitethroats go with all other warblers so
    regularly and so very far?

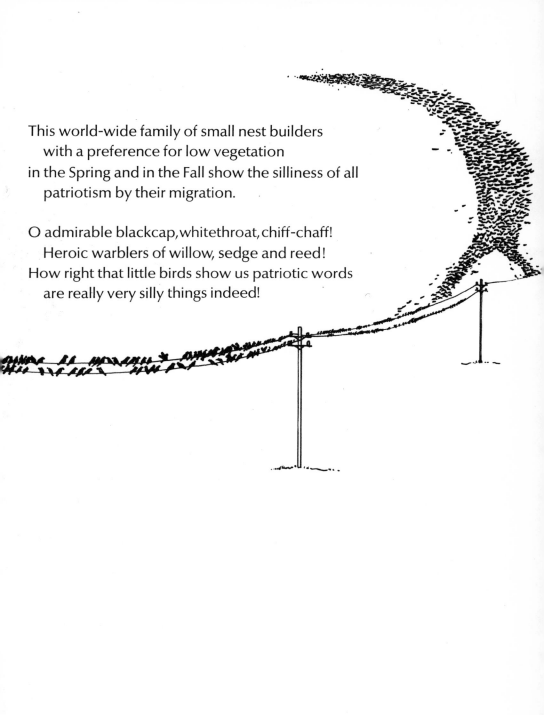

This world-wide family of small nest builders
   with a preference for low vegetation
in the Spring and in the Fall show the silliness of all
   patriotism by their migration.

O admirable blackcap, whitethroat, chiff-chaff!
   Heroic warblers of willow, sedge and reed!
How right that little birds show us patriotic words
   are really very silly things indeed!

XIPHIAS OR SWORDFISH

Xiphias is the Swordfish. He
is like a sword of light to see:
yes, like a fork of lightning the
swordfish flashing through the sea.
No Killer Whale or Tiger Shark
drives so dazzling to its mark
as Xiphias the Swordfish like
a finned and hissing marlin spike
strikes through a victim until it
hangs on his bright horn like a spit.
I have seen the Swordfish weep
tears of blood into the deep,
but that blood fell from the torn
Merman dying on his horn.

YETI, THE ABOMINABLE SNOWMAN

High in the Himalayan west, between Kanchenjunga and Everest
the Abominable Yeti sleeps within its icy nest,
   and the mountain climbers know
   the one footprint in the snow
(which falls every morning like divine confetti)
   is the largest, not the least
   indication of this Beast,
the Abominable Snowman, the One and Only Yeti.

When he bivouacks at night on the Himalayan height
with the iceface glaring bright and the Moon an eerie white,
   the mountain climber hears
   the sad howl assail his ears
of the solitary Yeti in the Himalayan night.
   Restless and afraid and sweaty
   all alone the only Yeti
trembles in his icy nest of sheer loneliness and fright.

Yes, the Yeti weeps all day as, high among the Himalayas,
a New Zealander, two Sherpas and, I think, two native Mayas
   seek out its icy nest
   on the heights of Everest
while the Yeti kneels and trembles at its prayers.
   It's not praying for its life:
   it is praying for a wife,
for even Yetis should exist in pairs.

ZONG NOT ZEBRA

You will think the Zebra
the last in the queue
of creatures I keep in
this Alphabet Zoo:
"What other animal,"
(I hear this said
in the silent schoolroom
of your head)
"is known by a name
that begins with Z?"
I must inform you
that you are wrong.
I speak now of the
sorrowing Zong.
The Zong is a vertical
fish who walks
on the face of the sea
as though on stalks.
He never descends
into the deeps,
he never (like other
fishes) leaps
into the sky

and he never sleeps:
he's a vertical fish
and so he keeps
walking on waves like
a broom as it sweeps
until out of sheer
weariness he weeps.
Then the tears of the Zong
fall into the sea
and the sea gets deeper
and deeper as he
wanders weeping incessantly
over the sea.
And when the Zong
rests his tearful eyes on
the morning line
of the World's horizon
and thinks he sees
an island rising —
O then the sorrowing
Zong in extreme
elation believes
it is not a dream.

Then he sees that his tears
like islands seem.
And: "The World is all water,"
the sad Zong cries,
"no lands and no islands
will ever rise
out of the seas to
greet my eyes.
I am alone on
a shoreless ocean
condemned to exist
in perpetual motion.
I'm lonely as only
a Zong can be
and I will drown
in the grief of me.
And so I sing
this farewell song:
O World! O Time!
It will not be long
before Zong sleeps
in the tears of Zong!"